The Fork-in-the-Road Indian Poetry Store

PHILLIP CARROLL MORGAN is an enrolled Choctaw/Chickasaw bi-lingual poet who has enjoyed a 25-year artistic collaboration with his painter-sculptor wife, Kate Arnott Morgan. This collaboration has seen the birth of three children, as well as the production of *The Fork-in-the-Road Indian Poetry Store*, which won the 2002 Native Writers Circle of the Americas First Book Award for Poetry. He has worked as a newspaper editor, business executive, building tradesman, guitar player, and rancher. He is currently a PhD student in Native Literature at the University of Oklahoma.

The Fork-in-the-Road Indian Poetry Store

Phillip Carroll Morgan

SALT

CAMBRIDGE

PUBLISHED BY SALT PUBLISHING
PO Box 937, Great Wilbraham. Cambridge PDO CB1 5JX United Kingdom

First published 2006

Printed and bound in the United Kingdom by Lightning Source

Typeset in Swift 9.5/13

ISBN-13 978 1 84471 267 0 paperback
ISBN-10 1 84471 267 2 paperback

TB

1 3 5 7 9 8 6 4 2

IN MEMORY OF RAYMOND WADE MORGAN

my father luak, *who held on to his chickasaw nation land, our home, despite the dawes commission, two world wars, the great depression, a period of alcoholism, three marriages and two divorces.*

Contents

Acknowledgments

Author photo by Joe Theige

Some of the poems, or versions of the poems, in this book have appeared in:

Georgetown Review: "Life's Work:"
                     "I Found the Earth in Snails"
                     "Snake Bags"
                     "We Spoke French Throughout the Desert"
                     "He Showed Them Snakes"

Soliloquy: "Ochre Hole"
Windmill: "On the Nile"
             "University Library"
             "Council Fire"
             "Flag of Mercy"

Pack River Magazine: "Stepping Out"

World Literature Today 2: "Anumpa Apesa a Iti Hikia: The Judgment of Standing Trees"

Choctaw Language and Culture : Chahta Anumpa. Marcia Haag and Henry Willis (Norman: U of Oklahoma Press. Vol.2, 2006):

    "Aiena e-Taloa: We Sing Together"

The creation and flood myths in "The Story of the Seeds" are drawn from oral tradition and from John R. Swanton's, Source Material for the Social and Ceremonial Life of the Choctaw Indians (Bureau of American Ethnology, 1931).

The author greatly acknowledges Lawrence Ferlinghetti's "Junkman's Obligatto," for the line, "full beard of anarchy," used in "Revolutionaries."

Special thanks to George Oliver for friendship and inspiration, to Janet McAdams for instruction and counsel, to Geary Hobson for elder wisdom and his immeasurable contribution to Native American literature, and to Katie and Ann Morgan for eternal encouragement.

perhaps a bit of fishes' fin
perhaps a bit of fish is I

—GEORGE VALODIN OLIVER, 1974

We, your grandparents still live,
our darts, our weapons are still powerful,
with them we brought glory to our people.

—AXAYAYCATL

POET AND LORD OF TENOCHTITLAN, 1474

Part I. Facing East

Having the need to pray
I come to the water's edge
where dawn light spreads out
                    over the riverbank
like a blessing of hands.
   An undertow of grief
lost in fragments of dreams
                    broken on rocks
carries me calmly
          into the eddy.
   I face the east
and breathe gently to the sun.

                    — *Geary Hobson*

Construction

words are crude materials
to build things with

do you
agree
strongly agree
mildly disagree
strongly disagree

Council Fire

i am looking at the chairs
empty of the friends
that shared my fire friday night
traces of their vigor
and clear images
of their being
linger here still

the elegant egalitarian
african the gentle attentive
ojibway the choctaw philosopher
the laughing scotsman
with bach and chopin
floating in his head
the cosmopolitan women
guarding their mysteries
with grace and intelligence
the american boys
exhibiting their fresh knowledge
of the interdependence
of all things the insightful swede
and the sociable eastern europeans
the affectionate knitting fusion
of young oklahomans
the kashmiri princess joking
with the gregarious muslim
and talkative jew
the *chilaki toba* (adopted cherokee)
who knew the names of flowering trees
and the beautiful native girl
who has forgotten her tribe

it started as a bonfire
in the newest firepit in the natural circle

of old leather-leafed oaks and mammoth hackberries
when the wood burned down
provided by the overburdened shade tree
wind and lightning had struck and split
we cooked over the coals shared
fragrant smoky food
and drank fancy beer

i see their faces illuminated
by the flames in the black night
i hear their voices in songs the memories
of their smiles are my money i spend it
more freely now i make regular donations
to my favorite charity the Human Unity Club

a young doe emerged from the woods
as i gazed at the chairs
around my firepit this morning
and saw my friends gracious
vistas around the fire
she strolled inside the perimeter
of my grass sampling
the leaves of young trees
she will remain in these woods for
their protection during this
bright aqua blue-skied day
with its okra blossom clouds
i studied her for a few minutes
as i sat down with my pen and journal
before the first word touched paper
she reminded me
that we can live together in peace
if we find value in it

flag of mercy

i am sorry for the white flash
of american anger
and pungent grind
of arabesque will
in hiroshima nagasaki new york
let's rid the world of evil we said

readers i say to you that i hate hate
against white
spangled terrors under any banner
or olive blouses

listeners know that i do not cry for
that fulfilled outcry would result in
perfect blind justice for myself or my nations
my own instantaneous end

worshippers know that my vitreous tears
for floral peace and perfect provender
are sincere when i pray
to stop starvation of my neighbors

know that my god hears
and does not welcome hatred of any
your fervent prayers
luminous element of creation

mothers fathers brothers sisters
preferences practices quirks or beliefs
know your browns blacks whites
create no discrepancy for me

haters know that i do not hate you
to those who look like you
and do not metaphorize your crimes
your passionate agendas your flags

do not inflame me
all our blazing emotions
know that mercy encompasses
and extinguishes our differences

people we are infant lambs
seeking nourishment and protection
in the same human flock
staring at the same stars

in the same black night
under cadenced moon
growing in the same sad garden
under sanguine sun

Closer to the Moon

the farm kids and i
decided to drive to the college town
for pizza supper tonight
my idea

an interview with the poet laureate
replayed on npr

ignoring back pain
i'm flying through humid luxuriant countryside
in a japanese car
grinding up visions of tall grass prairie
while he makes perfunctory statements
about religion reads poetry about death
with no imagery
bland blank verse
alludes to the white house guest list
the lack of intellectualism in washington

i didn't want to hear it again
flipped the channel to rock n roll
noticed cattle grazing upward
on the big green hill
i call the regional divide
the highest point between washita
and south canadian river drainages
an orange clay road
cuts a mile long "s"
up the mountainette
orange cutting green
vanilla cutting chocolate

is he colorblind? josie asked
about the man wearing a bright green
plaid shirt an orange plaid sportscoat
and butterscotch colored slacks
at the campus corner pizza parlor
he was bewhiskered middle-aged
i answered think again by raising my eyebrows
does he think he's cool?
asked josie probing deeper incredulously
he is cool i replied there's a difference
after the farm kids
finished competition at the pizzeria
(with the university silhouetted in the background)
to see whose eyes crossed deepest
and after strolling down the strasa
of boutiques and bistros
we disembarked to de-urbanize
and re-ruralize

    it was dusk thirty
    when we achieved the highway
    to retrace the vector
    across the divide
    the moon hung in the night blue sky
    entirely outlined but with only one eighth
    of its surface illuminated
    giving it a pronounced oblong
    almost pumpkin shape
    mercury glistened a few degrees south
    we sang songs with the radio
    all the way back the farm

josie was in the dummy seat
and as she stretched closed
the barb wire gate
i focused again on the spring tide moon
we had driven only nine miles
but I was taken
with how much closer we seemed
a couple thousand miles
closer to the moon

Ceremony

rooked crows talking all at once
at sunrise
like unruly school children

unlike songbirds speaking to each other
intervals of call and response

i stopped making coffee
went outside to listen

peachy glow eastern late summer sky
impressionist's blush over treeline

i squawked with them
five minutes non-stop
listening for human reply

none talking together
or to each other
at first light

save stockbrokers

More Like Children

```
            we
             live
            more
             like
            c h i l d r e n
            at  our house
            than      most
            people    do
```

we built it ourselves	men women children
with our own hands	without contractors
no mortgages	in a forest
squirrels and chickadees	for building inspectors
house has a built-in	ladder from an upstairs
bedroom to the	downstairs bathroom
the other bedroom	upstairs is accessible
and egressible by	way of a climbing rope
someone called it	a cross between swiss
family robinson	and peewee's playhouse
our house is built	with antique (salvaged)
lumber doors windows	sinks tubs faucets so it
is not very	energy efficient
but the air	is always fresh
some spiders and other	insects live in our house
they stay pretty much	out of our way because
we are bigger than they are	we like them lots more
than we like poison	it does not bother us
that the house is not finished	because neither are we

Holhpokunna the Garden of the Bumblebees

he protected and fed
the *vlla lawa* children
    an artisan crawling through
    the bathrooms of the rich
    making mosaics
        materializing
        material phantoms of desire
        receiving their praise
        receiving their scorn

intimately observing
katakshi komunta
the dread curse
that what they have is never enough
    he has handled hundreds of thousands
    of their holy dollars
    never cheating or failing to pay workers
    tax collectors
    insurance wasps

        now the children protect themselves
        and their children

no longer a stolen moment for a poem
a blooming black-eyed susan
but many hours swift flight
the beating of diaphanous wings

    his work now fields of rich clover
    coneflowers plum blossoms
    oak tassels primroses
    to crawl inside purple
    white orange yellow and black

                    and hear the songs of his kind
                    in the haystack nest
                    or earthen burrow
                    many hours sweet succulence
                    to taste pollenous sugars
                    of *holhpokunna* his dreams

to dine symbiotically
in *osapushi imosini*
the garden of the bumblebees

Mixed Blood

billy dan called
loaded on lithium
as i strode toward the door

if i hadn't stopped
to play one more song
on the piano
i could have avoided the call

billy's mother
is born of scotch clans people
and polynesian fishermen
his grandfather
mr willy
the last cherokee medicine man
in his arkansas family

billy's *keetoowah* dad sergeant charlie
once killed buddhist monks
offering sanctuary in their temple in Laos

billy like me grew up
in the black hole gravity
of oklahoma city
he's still incarcerated there
by the razor sharp guillotine
in his blood lines

finally off the phone
i drive away momentarily
from the knowledge of anguish
surfing asphalt lines
through wooded hills

to nancy's café
the exact point urban influence vanishes
dibble oklahoma
see men
framing a house in fair weather

buy the fifty-cent
city paper for a quarter
eat my breakfast
drink my hot black water

before thunder and lightning
summon me to drive
back home by backroads
slowly changing
from white man to indian
like eroding wood

wandering across
chickasaw lands
once owned
by my kin

it is a hard rain in january
a hard
clean rain

Mother *Yakni*

veined skin is thin
on your hands
wise bones that distinguish
our specie show their shape
compassionate eastern moon hangs in
pale blue late afternoon sky
over a low thunderhead
flashing lightning

my sun rising in your eyes
is looking back at itself
riverbottom valleys
between your knuckles are taut
singing is still heard there
the minerals are mine
flowing in the blood

i asked you about the hook
in your nose
you said jewish
straightfaced
in alabama i asked

you prayed me through
swift streams
the death and the burial
chilantakushi
acorn
stone
white sheets hung
in red dusty air
over bleached blonde prairies
the held clothes pins
the overturned coffee table

legs straight up
the ship
samanta
the haven
the rest

yakni = the land
chilantakushi = woodpecker eggs
samanta = the peace

The Great Society

flutter of wings

        through the wavy glass
        in kate's studio
            a tiger moth? a late-season monarch?

no   too cold

            my radar eyes lock
            on the wire of the hanging lamp
yes
tail-upturned securely grasping the precarious wire aero-gymnast
        house wren

deft hop to the sash
    then the doorway
        with missing threshold
            slipping out to flight
                moving through a ¾" crack without
                    so much as mussing a feather

the brief wrencounter   made me realize birdfeeders
were empty   an insult
to my friends   of color claw and beak

        announcing
        gave forth
        my best cardinal whistle

        who says
        there's no free lunch?

ah
the great society
the titmice re-con patrol   just zoomed in and out
soon a flash   of vigilant red
a dash   of squawkish blue
some elegant gray   and snowflake white

          saturday morning

flutter of wings

Rain Dancers

these

old blackjacks

go deep

in kiln hot weather

they seem unscathed

thin leathery leaves

stiff but supple

grasses around them

wither in the swelter

and change to blonde dust

must have a long taproot
                    some means
                    of finding
                    hidden
                    moisture
                    to endure
                    beardown
                    heat while
                    the hot dry
                    air changes
                    every liquid
                    particle
to vapor

The Carpenter's Dilemma

I

the fourteenth disciple
his own son
began in his tenth year
a glittering lad
with gifts

perhaps he was the one

in the beginning lessons
the young boy learned like breath
the native language of trees

the obscenity of flaw
was not possible
in the precision
of his conversation
with the trees
and the things he made with them

II

to surprise them
the master kept secrets
revealed
with episodic certainty
like the bone of a tiny fish
in the gums of a patron

a fleece of boring tools
rolled in a scrap of fine cotton cloth
which might appear like sent angels
in the chaos

odd oratories like
it's not raining boys
during furious downpours

in those songless rains
the apprentices worked unexpected chores
like caressing
tenderloins of wood
one hundred years old

revealing nursling smooth grains
double aged amber and ashen
born again in a cradleboard

III

the master had always wished
within the rubble of culture
for a female apprentice
to balance creation

but none had lingered
more than a laconic span of moons

he wanted to lead
but enjoyed no steps
in the ancient dance
of the woodlands

IV

the master understood perfection
but the broken blade
could not plane away
the defect

the wombless feminine
in his work

the one whipping of the son
the mother in-between
reminded him

that sap in wood
moves like the germ of acorn
in winter

that wax on the cradleboard
conceals fault
for only a century or two

like a full moon over a thunderhead

in the east
                    in a buoyant blue
                    late afternoon sky
i see your imagination

as a people
                    you rise early
                    you are visible
even the light of the sun
cannot burn you off

                    through a dark night
you are there
on the other side of earth

                    the glare of transplanted cities
                    cannot hide your agriculture
your stories
your flare for oratory

                    you speak
                    you listen
you persevere

The Fork-in-the-Road Indian Poetry Store

I.

i saved my energy as i read,
      like managing held-breath underwater
so i could extend my survey
      and not miss anything great

the fork-in-the-road indian poetry store
on the highway on the northeast side
of wetumka toward weleetka
      large open grassy field behind it
      county road completing the fork
      vanishes in verdant
      north oktahutchee bottomland
i am overcome
by the indianness of this town
                  exhilaration
                  an unexplainable import of joy
                  pervades me
even the few current-age vestiges
do not belie
                  a sense that this town
                  this people have always been here

II.

the reading today on the lawn is by two elderly sisters
in long gingham dresses who are the last living speakers of yuchi
you can stand still on an aisle inside the store and reach poems
and stories on the shelves in muskoke chikasha chahta and english

all the great indian writers on both sides
of the sweet gum bridge
      rich treasures of people
      alive and well on this continent
      after millennia of continuance

potluck table for reading guests
spread with banaha sofke tanfula
corn soup tobi squash and peppers
    brown-skinned teenager
    corner easy chair
    absorbing the story of an epic
    stickball competition
which attracted four hundred contestants
and twenty thousand spectators
    while columbus
    still navigated in an italian gene pool
    a century before his birth

  III.

the building
a turn-of-the-twentieth-century gas station
   abandoned for that use
   before model a's and t's
   disappeared from the road
     has weathered wood clapboard siding
     and two tapered wood columns
       on top of stucco pedestals supporting a roof
       which forms a one-car portico

honeysuckle perfumes
summer evening air while
   cicadas and tree frogs
   serenade well-dressed people
   sipping iced tea
     long shadows massaging
     green grass

a grandfather
plays a wood flute
    oddly harmonious
    with ratcheting locusts
dark-haired boys and girls
further east
    on the lawn revolve
    around a foam rubber football
        their cries forming another
        stratum of sound

IV.

what words would I write
if my favorite pen were the only pen left
in the world
and it held only a few drops of ink
i would write this
    in the creek *talwa*
    muskokean peace town
    corn sings harvest
        bluegills broom red sand
        with their tail fins
        in shallow kingfisher pools
        nearby people drumming
            a seated grandmother
            with a light spot on a brown iris
            in a wrinkle-supple face
            looks east through the yard
praying thankfully
and sees her grandmother walking
amongst children playing ball
you are welcome here

Part II. Turning North

Those few stars in the north seem so close.
Maybe they are right above Buffalo Pass.
Underneath the stars, the Lukachukai Mountain
lies dark and quiet. It breathes with the sacred wind.

—LUCI TAPAHONSO

Ochre Hole

ochre hole of urine two
feet deep in snowshoe
rabbit tracks a pause
to pee in winter's claws
and hear a breeze cause
laden trees to crack

then chase a grouse who
flapped and fluttered flew
the silence snapped raw
drought of freezing air paws
the frightened quarry through
bright narcotic slack

Revolutionaries

gloria
belle star of the northwest
introduced me a few days earlier to
mysterious juanie minooku from chicago
we hit it off

air was always nebular and cool
in those uplands
the old man from iowa
had called beautiful but treacherous
we all rode together
an extraordinary assemblage
along katka's mountain edge
that afternoon in an open jeep my full
beard of anarchy blowing in the stiff headwind

acquaintances of gloria the cabin buyer prospects were
a quiet radically dressed woman who occasionally
answered voices that no one else heard
and her violent husband
of basque origin
raised in oregon backwoods
who responded outlaw
dead serious
when asked
what he did for a living

it was on that road
that juanie turned
holding her hat
dark hair whipping her cheeks
and in her cartoon-toned
svelte voice
respectfully gave me
the nickname
fidel

The Big Woodpecker

a
call
well
noted
muted
c r o w
the big
woodpecker
perched in a high
pine maybe 200
yards through
snow-dense
w o o d s
bent on a
closer look
i crunched
a few steps
woodward
nosedown
curious dogs
at my feet but
night approaching
turned me back to the
neighbor's house for the
journey home an icy drive
and   long   walk   with   the child

would have me   home before dark
odd apprenticeship   as if my mentors
were always with me   guiding my footsteps
from great mississippi to   canada from canada to
baja to the   small   café in   san felipe that was so poor

to the bay where
sarah swam with
other native
children
in salt
water
warm
as a
bath

when you see the unforeseeable

there's a quickening in the blood
that's hard to explain
not adrenaline
more like the serum response
to meeting a new friend
in a place you've never been
who seems strangely and
profoundly an old friend

some call this remembering
what would i call it?

re-inventing yes discovering the familiar
geography you have never seen somehow you
know you've been sent to re-invent yes
recognizing immediately
the unknowable
and unforeseeable

Diphthongs to Dipterons

cabin conversation ranged
    and roamed
        from the competition
            of diphthong and literal vowel

pronunciation in southern states
    to the dozens of species
        of biting dipterons
            in minnesota

my recitation of closer to the moon
    and the desert love poem
        begat recitation in perfect french
            of andre breton poems

then their perfect english translations
    which begat haiku-like
        recitals of original
            poems in choctaw

and blossoming commentary on how
    each language changed the identical
        poetic impulse into dramatically
            different expressions

Stepping Out

Come up for ice skating, the telephoned invitation said. Joe, Kathy and their boys, Sarah's friends, lived at Dawson Lake way up on Meadow Creek Road. Sounded pleasant enough to a southern great plains river bottom boy—ice skating on the picturesque lake dug by a glacier in the Selkirk Mountains.

The cold transparent waters had shown us secret treasures in other seasons, like the native cut-throat trout in spring, with its speckled iridescence and crooked red line below its gill, a holy fish. We swam with it and the others on warm summer days; picnicked lightly on alluvial beach. Once in fall, we saw a young moose there, feeding in the shallows.

Ice echo-cracking like thirty-aught-six shots, and stressed moaning as the moon tugged at the foot-thick slab along the fault lines, struck timid fear to my soul. I was not prepared for the awesome presence of three hundred acres of living ice tensely flexing, like a being with one life, like a sea monster confined in a rocky crater.

My faith was in Joe as my popping ankles followed him onto the monster's back. Focus on the fearful cracking and groaning gave way soon to an exhilaration not since matched. It is not unusual to be inspired by white nicks in the ebony sky anywhere on this earth you are lucky enough to get a clear black night. But once I got my legs sufficiently to glide over that sleek floor, the stars came alive in a swaying motion. They zigzagged rhythmically in the generous heavens, and we danced the night away.

New York

we understand your travail
what it is like to lose thousands
of our people in a season
america we know how it feels
to be identified as enemy

our warriors always answered your calls
we chahta never fired upon you as a nation
my family's warriors have fallen
by your hand and by your side
we understand your sorrow

samanta chi-khanachi
may you know peace

Earth Life

got a little summer breeze heater
in the tool room of the barn
that my apprentice and i built last fall
got a salvaged slightly-cupped
age-weathered
extra-wide
pine board for a writing table
where i struggle
to round off the edges
of these words which cling
to the paper
like sticktight burrs to my socks

table rests
in pale winter light
channeled through the window
salvaged from a wooden hangar
they tore down at an airfield

on the endwall of the small room
the comforting durable old piano
i searched for
and found
at the countryside junk store
looks over my shoulder
like a shadowing grade school mother

the window opens onto
an old growth prairie oak forest
contrasted this bloodless january day
by a carpet of fine snow
grasses look flash frozen
where their stiff gray-blonde stems
protrude through the powder
like the bristling yellow hair of an ancient

i yearn for winter to cry out
but nothing is profound today
just cold
the statuesque cows
the silent birds
i had to cut some extra firewood
standing on plywood to keep my feet dry
put on two pair of long underwear
inspired by eight degrees and a north wind
a hot water pipe froze at the kitchen sink

i'm happy that my homespun
house does not strive toward
an illusion of perfection
happy that i cannot ignore the weather

i enjoy gathering fuel for heat
from hoary wise deadfall
in this crosstimbers grove
or immature greenwood
that complains alongside the road
when the utility people cut trees
in the right-of-way
i like having to do
a combination of things right
to keep my well water from freezing

it's a colorless day
argued with the wife
for no particular reason
early winter stress spent the whole day
in the house together yesterday

i love this life
life on planet earth
i hated planet metro and planet automatic
no struggle
no reward for struggling there
only a monotonous sense of uniformity
no beginnings no endings no triumphs
no natural catastrophes no entertainment
only perversion and stimulation

this earth life is my road
it's unpredictable
there's no map
no hocus pocus suggestion
that i am almighty

because i'm the only one
who has ever lived my life
i must travel the trail expectantly
it comes off trite to say
that even dullness is perfect
the excellence and symmetry of
winter and dormancy

are hard things to express
like the beauty of sleep
or the beauty of death
but any lesser view of cycle and rhythm
seems childish
foolish even

Endangered Species

herds of buffalo
gone now
                    you search the undulating
        sea of grass
near campo and wildhorse
                    for the great hairy horned whales
but none surface

instead
if you look carefully

                    you see the shallow swimming
        hahe issi
the pronghorn
antelope
                    you identify with
        this striped sailfish
skimming the surface
                    a harpoon's throw away
        from hungry nesters

diving
                    for the cereal great plains
        plankton seed
visible
but fast

Wooden Railroad Bridge on the Kootenai River

duck rifling two feet overwater
   poignant dream
      brown debris floats
         in rain swollen river
            thick clouds blue gray morning sun
               lowering my line into icy wind

floats as a spider casting off
   shimmering thread
      invisible winds
         like mouse teeth
            drive me inside to a chair
               there is no warmth for fishing

Hyphenated Winter

it may sound oxymoronic but
i never had a car wreck
while driving recklessly

all were low speed light traffic
asleep-at-the-switch mishaps

like this asleep-at-the-switch winter
no snow no ice no crystallized air

a cruel eight day span in january
featured six hours of sunlight
here in the sunbelt
six hours
the whole human population
turned to larvae
no moon or starlight either
el nino
the cloud i called it
like something
from the old testament

in march after planting onions and lettuce
came the killing freeze
out of context
an asleep-at-the-switch winter

today
we're into the second
non-stop day of soaking rain
beautiful and warm
but hard to negotiate with
i saw two quail collide
during last night's deluge

but not-to-fear
move a log or leaves
and see new bright green sprouts
germinations and gyrations of spring
none-too-soon to say good-bye to
the-winter-that-never-was

University Library

how dramatically
it diminished me
the first time i saw the insides
of a university library
row upon row
floor upon floor
of books
of books
of books
how could anything i write
or think
or do
possibly matter

i am older now
the university library
still diminishes me instantly
but I have learned to appreciate
diminishment
my own lack of importance
significance
centrality

Run

i see it
in my indian students' eyes
the impulse to run
i see it in myself
the impulse to run
from their schools

Water Planet

yellow-paged paperbacks
my sheath of wounded poems
sole companions

> but water
> through the window
> of a house
> on the flood control lake

a desolate planet
too far for scopes
where old people died
and younger people renovate
why did i agree
to give them this winter
of my loyalty?

awaken on a cot by the window
the only furniture
      musing on the significance of water[1]
brother wind stirring and whipping
      the reticent lake into whitecaps
water meringue pie

---

[1] *tinkle of small falls*
on slick red rocks in composting forest
roar of canadian snowmelt crick
as they say

the lying surface of water
deeper intrigue
whales leeches mud
invisible bow breaching rocks
shipwrecks
river bottom earth meat odors
the relationship between my body
72% water and
the external water
the living water
rain

Winter Trees

winter trees
out my window again
nearest neighbor
needs a good set of binoculars
to see me naked

the trees are naked
strong trunks skinny limbs
like teenagers
i watch them change
each season

framed statically
in the bedroom glass
light comes up slowly
each morning
out that west window
like stage lighting
i wake up with it
no alarm

you can see beyond
winter trees
no leaves to conceal
nesting fledglings
all have stumbled
from the nest
eaten by predators
or found their wings

I Have Some Advice For You

I.

like an armadillo for insects
the poet constantly
grubs for words
that will delight an audience
never quite open to definition

the painter strives
for the sublime image
and stroke
that will burn itself
into the collective eye
of the western world

they each
meet their mother
as a child
before she dies

II.

i do not have
crows in my eyes
spiders are not warming
in my sleeves
grandmother has crows
in her eyes
and spiders in her sleeves

talk to her
do not let her
follow the crows

III.

i have some advice for you

use hackberry
for your fall fire

start it with the smoke
of cedar and pine
look into the amber flame
but not too long
it can burn your eye

pinch and sprinkle east
some tobacco
burn some for smoke
but not too much
it has power
and you must learn
to live with powerful things

use the hackberry
falamma north wind
in spring broke over
and offered you
for this fire

be thankful
you know this

IV. *(the deer sonnet)*

i hit a deer
issi achukma
on the way to work
this morning

trembling
i opened the car door
with light footfalls
approaching the motionless doe

yaya chants
of the deer dance
rang in my head
as i knelt to touch her

she raised her head and said
don't be late for work

V.

i am indian
i am chahta

i do not eat chocolate
it is too sweet

the ancestors
did not eat spicy food

i want to be skinny
like the white people

VI.

i have some advice for you

do not start your fire
with pages
from your pornography book

they are too slick
and cold

VII.

you can see things
when you commute
especially in the dark
after working late

you can hear things
like the *shawi*
like the raccoon
playing in the shoulder grass
on two consecutive nights
in the same place

she says
don't run out and get hit
like *ofi* and *issi* did
like coyote and deer did
on september twelfth

Part III. Facing West

I travel from a tribe whose name bears storm clouds
and enter a country where a drink of water
is a way to pray

—JOY HARJO

The Two-pronged Stick

a hickory branch green
good for night-roasting fish
you peel back the bark and cut it
at the fork a tempting dish
is smoked at the end of a stick
you sit close enough to hear
orange cracklings and the scaled skin
bubbles gray-white and clear
up to the blackened spiny fin
redrock holds the fish head's eye
watching body unto body
and black crows cry

Father *Luak*

i see him
in the blackjack coals
straight line
of his lips
the hat
lizard skin hands
thick toenails

black stripes on his cheeks
reveal sorrow
plus determination
to survive
forsaken
quenched
abandoned and confused

he and brother *mali*
swam the length of lake
underwater
without a breath
rising a tornado
to inhale
the dust
and spare wooden houses
nesters had spun

yaya crying
fed not his sorrow

luak = fire
mali = wind
yaya = mournful

World's Largest Rez

I was born and raised in the world's largest Indian reservation, Oklahoma. In 1342 (A.D.) God came to all Indian prophets in a dream and told them to warn the people: "okla hish asha tohbi-vt miti-achi (the white hairy people are coming)." The people ignored the prophets so God created a whale and named it Oklahoma.

He then encoded European devils to send the nations to the whale, which swallowed them. They also sent Norwegians and Russians and Welshmen and Irishmen to be swallowed by the whale. Then, in case the whale inadvertently coughed us up, the U.S. sent Englishmen and Germans to stand guard and kill us if we emerged. But what Uncle Sam didn't know was that Indians invented English and Germans (and, of course, Norwegians Russians, Welsh and Irish) and that they had no real power over us.

So when all was digested (it took several hundred years for such a large meal), God changed the whale into an Indian, who had, of course, digested the Europeans. The joke once again was on old Uncle Sam because now he had millions more Indians to deal with, many of whom were invisible and silent, until we awakened them with our words.

Journal Entry: March 23rd, Chihuahuan Desert

river shade
    of nicotiana tree
    glinting hummingbird
    sampling precociously
    spare blossom nectar

    campfire dried leaves smoked
        amid talk of eating roots
        of sotol
        lechuguilla
        living rock cacti

        cane stalk flute and whistles whittled
            bamboo surrounding
            the dusk of
            unknown hot springs

            ten paces
                from the emerald river
                in this desert wild place

        gigged catfish sizzles
            on a spit
            offering itself
            by flute music
            in the whiter light of morning

            side canyons
                where no water is
                water polished purple granite
                smooth as gizzard stone

hummingbird hovers
        reading my journal again
        while my head rests
        on smooth green bark
        at a comfortably low
        fork in the tree trunk

        plea of feather
                fluttering wings
                touched my hair

Am I Seeing?

they go through the world
without seeing

        i know this is an old theme
        Grandfather
        but I must repeat it
        myself
        in order to see if i know it
        or if i just repeat it
        without
        knowing

peat-barked oaks
on the pacific side
of these california hills
make me feel secure

        the grass that looks like
        lions' fur on the inland side
        made me nervous

like some of the hellion
two leggeds that live here
have made me feel
descendants of the ones
who earned five dollar bounties
for each native
they could exterminate

the evil here
seems irresistible
Grandfather
it permeates everything
like coffee in a paper towel
they pass through all lands
as if all lands' spirits were the same
am I paranoid
or am I seeing
Grandfather?

they go through the world
without seeing

halito akhana
hello my friend

you have crossed
your dark river
dancing across
the sweet gum bridge
into the *tohwekelih samanta*
into the luminous peace

hello my friend
hash-maka anumpa chito
tell us the whole story

tell with sharpest vision
the meaning of journeys
of gambling the bone game

we see you
tossing flies
you've tied
into the clearwater stream
leaning back
on the smiling
waving
grass

Ballad of Kenneth Ruth

like tom joad's
wrathful grapes
kenneth ruth shot
jeffrey windham
in self defense

a poor okie
whose reports to police
were ignored
about stolen food
from the shared tenement frig

windham blundered in
in the middle of the night
the drunk boy who'd soon be dead
he was belligerent and rude

from his room next door
ruth heard him kicking in
wilson's door

ruth wondered whether
to stand or run
he loaded up his twenty two gun

he warned windham
windham charged
it took four shots
to make the drunkard fall

cleveland county convicted ruth
manslaughter first degree
put him in a penitentiary cell

ruth still asks
what was i supposed to do
i guess next time I'm robbed
i'll shoot myself

Anumpa Apesa a Iti Hikia:
The Judgement of Standing Trees

chafichi- driven

by august firebreath
from the field work
we taste millennia
without air conditioning
on southern plains

takchaka honayo- at the wild edge

of streaming water
whispering songs
red-belly woodpeckers drum
we rest like brothers
father and son
face up
on damp gravel
in red cleft of creekbank
upon cool vulva of earth

e-hokupa- we are stealing

the musky bed
of bobcat and badger
so righteous trees
willow and cottonwood

simoachi- paint dark slender stripes

and moving spots
upon our skins

Click Beetle

thin shadow cast by a
phosphorescent click beetle
enigmatic emblem
of canyon drumming

    rain varnished limestone
    granite echo
    men outliving the extinction
    of their souls

moon tracks clear across
timeless black canvas
ancestors studding
a canopy of hope

    lightning bleached
    supercharged air
    stinging nostrils
    with firefly life

escaping death
the river road
pulsing click of current
unites us we survive

Life's Work

1. *I Found the Earth in Snails*

a friend of snakes first published at sixteen
in the herpetological journals
a multilingual poet when we met

you took me to the wichita mountains
the sacred stones
and we dug friendly
with sticks and fingers for
tiny white snail shells
and then replaced them
inseparable universes
as you described the layers of living earth
in english and latin

i was a fearful child
embalmed in disjuncture
the ennui gap collapsing in a contagion
of your verve

you knew the lichens
all things living here
the miniature dinosaur schiloperos
and an asexual lizard
that cloned in the crevices of these boulders

against the rules we camped in a lithic cluster cave
under the raven canvas needlepoint stars

before we erased our traces the next dawn
we breathed smoke into the fire of cedar
sipping well water from one canteen
and beaujolais from another
eating prickly pear and laughing

11. *Snake Bags*

On that blistering spring day, canoes were laden with drinking water, food, camp gear, equipment and a guitar for the 12-day river trip into the desert canyons, one of the few remaining true wildernesses near the 30th parallel in North America. The morning after the first night thunderstorm had us navigating a flood-stage current, which disguised frightening new channels from main channels.

A driftwood debris stream flowed down the center of the water-way, a knot faster than our canoe. From the debris flow Jorge lifted out a belly-up rattlesnake, which he laid in the floor of our pirogue. I told how the Chahta hold the diamondback in high regard because it protects the corn supply from scavenging rodents.

Is it alive, I asked? No, but the one under your bench is, he replied, with a cautious grin. And the two under my bench are alive, he added . . . in the bags. In the hasty broil of loading the canoes I had wondered why he had not put the burlap bags in the gear-safe watertight pickle buckets, but fatigue wiped out the question before I could ask it. We had driven an eternity around the un-roaded, uninhabited desert region just to reach the put-in point at Maravillas.

Jorge was not a typical zoologist, though he possessed more scientific knowledge than anyone I had ever met. He loved and respected the animals he studied. Unlike his university colleagues, who embalmed them in jars of formaldehyde, Jorge's snakes had lived in relatively comfortable terrariums, sharing his apartment for the past year. He returned the snakes to the exact places he had captured them and released them back to their homes.

III. *We Spoke French Throughout The Desert*

from his sunglasses
was a young man
confident to the edge

i was unsure the tires
could survive miles and miles
of cruel stony unmapped road

the wheel darted quickly
his hands and arms following again

breath was dry
a desert air
    bound west
        through accented jars
        we were carried quite distant
        memory of water
        was at best elusive

we were so far out
the past petrified
like a war scene
chiseled in relief
on the wall of a tomb

between us we knew eleven languages
so we used a kind tongue
to balance a sun so hot
lizards lay in the crevices of history

                        his eyes still wandered
                        with soil old
                        intent on purpose
                        to some rock or european girl
                        i suppose

we lived
and died there
without ceremony
in a world we could not own

IV. *He Showed Them Snakes*

In southwestern Oklahoma the splendid Wichitas rise from great
plains shortgrass like righteous temples of the Plains Tribes. The
Fort Sill military reservation desecrates a large portion of the
range with death machinery inside tall spectral wire fences. Early
in my apprenticeship, Jorge took me to the public access wildlife
'refuge' area in those mountains to further my friendship with
the earth.

At the sunny trailhead this holiday weekend we ate our lunch
preparing to disappear into the ancient tabernacles of mineral
and water. Three burr-headed GI's in civilian garb and their dates
picnicked nearby when a clamor of human hooves arose. Jorge
had just mentioned that he hoped we would see the coachwhip
snake, the fastest land creature hereabouts, when the three
soldiers sprung up, no match, to chase one to impress their
women shouting kill.

Jorge laid down his food, took three seconds of visual bearing and
joined the pursuit. With the darting agility of a roadrunner he
captured the whipsnake in his hands, clutching it like an
eggshell. He carried it to the picnic table where the wide-eyed
young women sat aghast, the confused men following in rank.

In a sympathetic baritone, he explained the nature of the animal,
as if describing a Van Gogh to art lovers. The ladies and gentle-
men listened blankly transfixed. With a slight lilt of discovery in
his voice he focused on his own tender fingers holding the
snake's midsection, remarking that the reptile had apparently
recently eaten.

With manual deft, and to the manifold astonishment of his audience, he gently massaged the belly and worked a just-dead lizard through the snake and out its mouth into his hand. After briefly describing the lizard he fed the whiptail delicately back to the snake, noting that this in no way harmed his friend, then released the snake at the spot where he had picked it up. We finished our lunch and nothing more was said.

most cynics would laugh

if i said life was a symphony
but i'm thinking specifically

                about the crescendos of zeal

and the regressions from zeal
in life

                we've all seen that

in work
in art
in love

                we all have a purpose

our legacy
our gift
our cross
our quest

sometimes quixotic
sometimes cathartic
always symphonic

                you may laugh

but you know what i mean

On the Nile

it could have been the nile
vanilla sands incased by
strata of chalky senna
boxed in canyon
built by little people
stacking crackers

we slid into the delirium bath
like dust slick salamanders
or river bottom sponges
backlit by a brush stroke wash
magenta fire of the sun

heroic figures
dragon fly surface dance
coffee colored river
scent of clay
suspended seed
urban refugees
bad memory war
lost in past

All About Wind

i climbed
to the summit
of the sandhill
sunrise view was commanding
of the family of sharp-crested dunes
and perfectly elliptical bowls
of sand fine clean sand
a few sand peaks touched
but did not eclipse
the skyline

symmetrical prints
of a small squirrel in
straight lines across the dunes
spider burrows and attendant sand piles
not yet erased by the wind

returning downhill to camp
i followed a perfectly parallel
line to my footsteps going up
out of regard to the flawlessly
concentric ripples in the sand
as if the erratic wind
somehow possessed immaculate rhythm
i concluded finally
that the sandhills
were all about wind
not about sand at all

as i looked back
toward the summit
during my retreat from it
i could see my footprints
on the highest slipface of the dune
from the lower elevations anyone
could have seen my imprint
from a great distance
a moment of personal glory
soon to be erased by the wind

On That Great Plateau

in southeast colorado
two buttes
rise up majestically
in a round treeless sea of grass

i'm still not driving
having given up the wheel
at the nuclear power plant
near cheyenne
i have never been able
to drive past that thing

in straight line of sight
with the two buttes
the ruined hacienda
stands a brother
befriending innocent birds

calls my name
each year i pass that way

hello it says
you passed the dream line

lead colored corral boards
hold the trace of horses
hoot of man

bright as birth
the white light glares
all the way through
that adobe sun house

live here it says
you passed the dream line

A Desert Love Poem

we were like two lizards
walking upright
with straw hats
with walking sticks
your sombrero had a stampede string
under your chin
and a wreath of silk flowers for a hatband
mine a gray cowboy style crown
all wrinkled crimped and shaped

i am a tinaha
(in the mexican sense)
all full of poems
an earthen jug filled
with metaphor simile rhyme
as we kissed at first light
my mouth was filled
with all the flavors of the desert
a tea of ocatillo leaves
sotol bulbs and resurrection plant

i am still not sure
what you are
the west texas wind
the northern mexico wilderness
a mountain lioness
surveying the big bend
in the rio grande
from her cave in the cliffs
a yucca bloom a creosote bush
the big dipper whirling
around the north star
in a black sky

you are an enigma
like the desert
an enchanting irresistible enigma
your pathways are compelling
but not marked
your combinations are endless
your beauties infinite
you are an intricately planned garden
your flora the champions
of the plant world

i am in every sense ignorant
your mysteries simultaneously
resolve and rebuild
my fascination increases
with every journey
into your wildness
into your peace
i am a cactus wren
darting between your thorns
i am the bear
drinking from your springs
the bee at your blossom
i am sand
healed by your winter
annealed by your summer
you are the desert
i am in wonder

Part IV. Turning South

Turn to the south
to the midday sun.
Feel the wind and
accept the innocence of trees.
Rise above
the disappointments of the past.

—LUCY OKCHIAH WADE

creator

did you think of every cut every angle
every pitch every slope when you created earth
did you carefully design the textures the color

scheme or rather did you simply command
the elements in great spontaneous tones
of orchestration and dynamic perhaps you just

set in eonic motion as the evolutionists suggest
the rain and wind and volcanic heat throwing
in an occasional asteroid impact or axis shift

should i fear your next whim of cataclysmic
genius i think not did the paint fear davinci's
brush the stone michelangelo's chisel the word

pushmataha's oratory i will not fear but ponder these
questions as i plot another day of cutting out my own
designs fitting the corners measuring the notches

gauging tolerances i will take heart in reckoning
how though i am insignificant my work somehow
fits in with yours your great masterpiece earth

The Story of The Seeds

hear me   listen i say
this is the story of the seeds

Prologue

the earth was a muddy quagmire
like clotting blood
produced in its chaotic state
by the power of the creator

who in the appearance of a red man
came down and made
a large mound nanih waiya
or sloping hill

he caused the red people
to come out of it and
when a sufficient number
had come out he stamped the mound
like thunder

when this sign of power was given
those who were partially formed
with only their heads
above the mud
all perished

the quagmire mud was boiling hot
in a state of great agitation
driven by violent winds
the soft mud was shifted
in various directions and
deposited in different places

i smoke
and drink coffee
wondering if anyone
will ever read this

will my audience
scoff a woman
saying hmphh
creator my eye

will she register
immediately
intuitively
how i struggled
with the spelling
of hmphh

will she understand
that the origin of all legend
is myth
and the origin of all myth
is legend

is the olive tree
of her people
more deciduous
than my hickory

with the earth thus fitted
for human habitation
the creator said the earth
would bring forth spontaneously
the chestnut hickory nut and acorn
for their subsistence

later corn was discovered
by means of a crow

will the map-maker's europe
condescend to permit
this song
of hot clotting mud

will she believe
that seeds
who flawlessly replicate
their ancestors tell history
more accurately than books?

1. *Dipper Gourd*

it is the spaniards' horses
riding down the corn
flashing most often
across my mind's eye

overtaking the smell
of blood and glimmer
of iron petals of swords
blooming in the sun

not hearing the bells
on the beasts of conquest
nor seeing the shining metal
the ghost-skinned hairy men
wear to cover their heads

hiding in the riverbank brush
of the mabila
hearing groans and screams
as one more is found

terror has my throbbing bones
grope for the dipper
still tied to my sash

i unlatch it silently
reach down for the water
sipping as if my last

all i can see
or hear
or smell
this morning

is spaniards' horses
riding down the corn

ii. *Vine Beans*

the bones the bones
how can we make so many bundles?
there's no time
the bonepickers are dead

they died with the 500
women children elderly
in each big house
burned like caddo buffalo prairie

where there were thousands
now there are tens
we wander speared
arrayed like seeds of beans
in the dust
half-circles of life
among the dead

the seeds the seeds
we must not flee without them
i see my cousin who no longer knows me
filling earthen jugs with seeds
lashed over his bloody shoulders

where are you going?
to the hills the soldiers may return
we will go toward black wisdom
to the bluebird mountains
they marched toward the winter
sinti hishitobah[2] has returned
remember the story of teotihuacan

---

[2] *the feathered serpent*

yes the ghost fire there
the emigration

i know the bones will be scattered
but still i can see the climbing beans
the summer corn
the granddaughters

III. *Squash*

my name is ilappa shua
i come from hashi aiitolaka
the west
to learn the mabila way
of keeping seeds and growing things
my mother sent me to live with her sister's boy
whom i had met to hunt with
several hashtulahpi autumns before
in the month of berries
i am instructed also
to study and bring home
a family of shoshi haksinchit abi
assassin bugs

my cousin and i are now among survivors
fleeing to the hills
though he seems not to recognize me
leaving behind the bones of his people
for three days we have walked without speaking
the stones we walk
no slick-footed
war beasts can travel
we sleep for a few hours each night
heads on our bundles
no fires

today we have found a large cave
and built a fire
i speak
telling a story
exactly as my grandmother
told it to me

the wailing cry was heard
coming from all directions
oka falamma oka falamma
the returned waters

stretching from horizon to horizon
it came pouring its massive waters onward
the foundations of the great deep
were broken up

soon the earth was entirely overwhelmed
by the mighty and
irresistible rush of the waters
sweeping away the human race and all animals
leaving the earth a desolate waste

of all mankind only one was saved
and that was the mysterious prophet
who had been sent by the great spirit
to warn the people of their near approaching doom
the prophet saved himself by making a raft
of sassafras logs by the direction of the great spirit

various kinds of fish swam around him
and twined around the branches of submerged trees
while upon the face of the waters
he looked upon the dead bodies of men and beasts
as they rose and fell upon the heaving billows

after many weeks floating he knew not where
a large black bird came to the raft
flying in circles above his head
he called to it for assistance
but it replied only in loud croaking tones
flew away and was seen no more

a few days after a bird of bluish color
with red eyes and beak came and hovered over the raft

the prophet asked if there was a spot of dry land
anywhere to be seen in the wide waste of waters
then it flew around his head
fluttering its wings uttering a mournful cry
before flying away in the direction
where the new sun seemed to be sinking
into the rolling waves of the great ocean of waters

immediately a strong wind sprang up
and bore the raft rapidly in that direction

soon night came and the moon and stars
again made their appearance
the next morning the sun arose in its former splendor
the prophet looking around
saw an island in the distance towards which the raft
was slowly drifting
before the sun had gone down
again into the expanse of waters
the raft had touched the island
upon which he landed and encamped
weary and lonely he forgot his anxieties in sleep

when morning came
in looking around the island
he found it covered with all varieties of animals
except the mammoth which had been destroyed
he also found birds and fowls of every kind
in vast numbers upon the island
among which he discovered the identical black bird
which had visited him upon the waters
and then left him to his fate

he recognized it as a cruel bird
he named it fulushto
raven
regarded as a bird of ill omen ever since

with great joy he discovered the bluish bird
which had caused the wind to blow his raft
upon the island and because of this act of kindness
he called it puchi yushuba
lost pigeon turtle dove

after may days the water passed away
and in the course of time
puchi yushuba became a beautiful woman
whom the prophet soon after married
and by them the world was again peopled

when i finish telling the story
i pour the flat white squash seeds
from my pouch into the palm of my hand

i see i say clustered in my hand
litoli pakanli lampko
lusty orange blossoms
i see i say na nihi yushuba
lost seeds
becoming beautiful mothers
i see i say okchamali hishi auata
broad green leaves
sheltering the fruit

IV. *Pumpkin*

two died last night in the cave
the moans and outcries at night
are the worst part

i heard coyote last night
singing to our surviving dogs
who know when to be quiet
even coyote was silent
the night of the attack
and the second night
with new men in the woods
on the backs of violent beasts

i'm sitting in the mouth of the cave
beside the watchers this morning
we are not speaking
listening to light rain
drip from overhanging rocks
where our dogs are sheltered

i have poured
into my hand
a few pumpkin seeds
from the innermost pouch
in my bag

we will eat bad food this winter
even spoiled meat perhaps
we will need every pumpkin seed
we can spare
for medicine

the spaniards took
our stores of corn

i stopped my pickup
when i saw the blue heeler pup
looking lost on stinson creek road
head up withers low
he came a few steps
toward the truck
i got out and we carefully
closed the gap between us

since blue took up the territory
around my cabin
coyote has set up the most raucous
songs i've ever heard at night
around here—first from dragonfly creek
on the east then from near woods west

"you're dead blue dog" he yips and taunts
"don't fall asleep" he laughs

"bring it on shadow dogs" blue barks
"my man and woman and i
will defeat you"

listening from my bed
i smile at this conversation
alert until the scent of light rain
drifting through my screen
sends me back to sleep
beside the strong warm woman
dreaming of my healers

v. *Corn*

the spaniards had surrounded lapalika town
where cousin nukshopa's aunt and uncle had lived
they killed everyone
the same day they destroyed mabila
nukshopa recognized a friend
among the dead
who had run from mabila to warn them
but not soon enough
he showed no sword wound
his head had been crushed
by a spanish war horse

we reach yushwihelichi
the priests' village
on the second day
they know nothing of the attacks
but flee with us
taking with them their stores
of food and seed corn
if we could make it through the winter
there was hope in the corn

with watchers posted in all directions
we eat bitter acorn bread
goosefoot seeds
squirrels duck turkey and fish
through the winter and spring

shilombish chito the great spirit
who had sent ikhana the observer
to follow the crow
and bring back the corn to the people
in a day no one living could remember
ensured our survival

the humma corn is my favorite
fresh or ground into bread
i remember mabila each time i eat
word has come that the sinti hishitobah
marched off with his slaves and devils
toward my mother's people
i fear for them but resist fear with faith
that the fast runners and boatmen
we sent to warn them succeeded

in council we agree
that we will no longer build large towns
until the white devils
are driven from our land

my neighbor the wheat farmer
asked me why i grow gourds
which i cannot eat
raising an eyebrow i did not answer
why do you go to church i asked him?
to worship god he replied
that's why i grow gourds i said

what i did not tell him
was that the gourds tell me
this story i have told you

yes they and the vine beans
and the squash the pumpkins
and the corn
tell me these stories
which they remember
and cannot forget

vine beans do not whisper
but shout in the spring
when they leap from the soil
of this earth our bed
uncoiling their strong necks
lifting their heads towards the sun
climbing to the moon each night

and the squash sing in summer
with loud voices
that they are of the earth
by the earth and for the earth
as their mammoth-ear leaves
shade the earth
and their life giving fruit

and the glad pumpkins
sound the comforting drum beat
as they spread once again
to celebrate in fall the summer harvest

and the dry corn in winter
laugh and dance in their jugs
as the fires of their people
burn brightly

yes this is the story of the seeds
a story of love and survival
yes i see i say i hear i know
this is the story of the seeds

No Goodbye

my heart sings as
a symphony of cicadas
                        spiraling straight up
like scissortails do
catching flies at dusk

feeling the minimal tug of gravity
as wings drive us straight up
then the buoyancy of the air
drifting down on currents
only to settle and spiral up again
                        gulf blue sky underlit with orange
                        an armada of shiplike clouds
                        above the horizon

my eyes welled with tears
straining seriously
to prevent crying out loud
departing my first lesson
in choctaw   my ancestral language
first words fresh on my tongue
overwhelmed like a lost dog
re-united with its master
like a slave freed and returned home

                        asked about parting gestures
                        my mentor replied
                        in chahta we have no word for goodbye

Anumpa Bok Lukfi Hilha
(Treaty of Dancing Rabbit Creek)

pi-pokni lawah
micha pi-mafo lawah-vt
yakni imposa-ttok
itikba peni fohki
bok boha chitoh akkahikah

fichi-lvknah-vt
ai ninak kolaha okchamali-lhiposhi
isht-alhpisa hikia okla-sahnoyechih
yakni-imposa-ttok
itikba akuchi hastula nowa
akuchi hina-chilukoah

chukfi lumah-vt hilha micha lobukachi-ttok

hvcha hinlatuk anufohkah-kiyoh
kanima okla-ilap-immih aia
lukfi lhali-tuk im-ibbak
nishkin okchi lawah yaya-ttok
hakta yakni chuka pisachukmah
anoa kiyoh pis-achi kanima im-oklah-vt
talhepa sipokni lvwa aiasha-ttok

kalampi-ttok issish bano-ttok
ahni-ttok illi-ttok
i-fonih-vt okla hummah isht ona-ttok
i-chabiha sitoha-fonih-vt
talli-tuk micha itamoa

amba chim-pisa
amtakla okchay-achi
im-boshulli micha im-tushtua-vt
okchah alichih
kia aiena anumpa lvwa
pa il-anumpilih

chukfi luma-vt hilha micha lobukahci-ttok

Treaty of Dancing Rabbit Creek
(Anumpa Bok Lukfi Hilha)

many of our grandmothers
and grandfathers
kissed the earth
before loading on the boats
to travel the big muddy river

light yellow stars
in the jade green magnolia night
stood watch as the old ones
kissed the earth
before walking out into the winter
into the broken road

the rabbit danced and fell into the creek

pearl river could not understand
where his own people were going
they cupped the dirt in their hands
they cried many tears
because they would never again see
our beautiful home land where our people
had lived for thousands of years

they froze they were bleeding
they suffered they died
their bones were carried to oklahoma
some of the bone bundles
were scattered and lost

but they see you
and live on through me
bits and pieces of them
awaken strengthen
even with these words
we are speaking

the rabbit danced and fell into the creek

The Dogs Did Not Follow

the dogs did not follow
as i started out
to walk in the woods
they are unruly and unkempt

> leaves are gone
> birds more visible
> a flicker skipped by

the dogs are used to running the range
without human reference
most of the time
left alone to their own devices
at our new home
on our old land
in the chickasaw nation

> transition to rural
> even after only one urban generation
> in hundreds
> is most difficult
> a great battle of psyche
> an agonizing labor as childbirth
> painful gestation
> breech birth

steam of summer has given way
to nakedness in fall
stripped stick figure trees
the bony dogs
my vocal chords relax into their depression
a human mourning dove cry
the dogs come running

sun hangs a marshmallow
in leaden morning clouds
dogs understood my howl
coming to my aid
a stampede of two

chimney blackjack smokescent
short sleeved chill
the dogs follow me back to the house

Black Crow

black crow
are you laughing at me?
crops come
crops go
children born
children die

wife
grows
old and
windblown

you stay the same in the sky

black crow
black crow
you got oily black wing

caw haw caw haw you sing

black crow
black crow
are you laughing at me?

The Lost Ponds

worried about my fishing boat
cold day but sunny
so wrapped up in work this fall
haven't been to the lost ponds to fish

the ponds are remote enough
just leave my little rowboat there
but still roaming fishermen
are efficient
someone may have just loaded it up
and carried it off

must go through two barb wire
gates and a third steel gate
a mile and a half off the county road
to reach the first lost pond

never see anyone there
but the beavers
who slap the water
with their shotgun blast tails
to scare me off
but in vain
since i bring them no harm

absentee landlord has given
me permission to fish there
a fisherman's dream
old ponds deep water
- - - - - - - - -

the little boat was still there
about half full of rain water
too heavy to even turn over
to empty so i wandered
along the banks
like the heron
to fish
so quiet not so much as a gum wrapper
or cigarette butt to spoil the attraction
will return with the boy another day
to fetch the boat

White Bone Hooks

i thought of the white bone hooks
the scholars dug
sacrilegiously out of the burial mounds

while fishing
           singing
                    praying
              bluegill
whiskerfish

i awoke on my cot to
      open summer sky
                no dew fall
     silent
oarfall

with the woman
         who
                loves
     to fish
and me

somewhere in my sleep
i'm sure
     i heard
            my white brother
     who lives inside me
say he was sorry

i dreamed my elder
the wordmaster
squatting on the creek bank
baiting a white bone hook
as i awoke the younger

Aiena e-taloa

We Sing Together

chilantakushi lusah micha tohbi-vt	small black and white woodpecker
iti hahe chaha binilih	sitting in the tall bare acorn tree
hochvffo	is hungry
ilimpa atalhi-li	i am preparing food
onish micha tachi kulloh	millet and hard corn
himak vpachi	then she will eat
hushi momah vpachi	all the birds will eat
bokoshe e-heli	we fly to the creek
oka kapussa il-ishko	we drink the cold water
hvttvk-e-taloa	we sing to the man
hvttvk-pim taloa	the man sings to us

"v" is a *Chahta* short "a"
pronounced like the "u" in hut.
The underlined vowels are nasal.
The "a" in *Chahta* is pronounced
like the "an" in sang; the "i" is
pronounced like the "in" in sing.

Meadowlark, Large Family of the Plains

orange stem buffalo grass a lone
oak ragged owl nest tall stump
red pond

"rool ry ah"   echo   "rool ry ah"

black collar triangle perching bird
calling wing meadow color unspotted
echo soft horizon caller

Ragged Owl Nest

ragged owl nest
remnant of rodent
absent hooter-fly
flat beak hook

winddrift stumpwood
silhouetted moondogie
ragged owl nest
remnant of rodent

A Popular Theme

as quickly as it occurred to me
i dismissed the idea
                    every time quickly
anyone can pick a common subject
like love i said and write a lyric
or song or prose piece
                    what about other
                    important themes and textures
                    like friendship history war spirit?

this poem is about love
about the puffy-faced smile of a
birth mother as she twines the fine
hair of the newborn infant who is instinctively
basking in the voluntary affection
and entire nourishment
of sublime nurturing breast
                    it is about that
                    same child decades later twining
                    the fine silver white hair of her
                    mother as the spirit slips freely
                    from her maternal body[3]

it is about the enlightening of
romance the breezy exhortations
of holding hands and kissing

---

[3] which has been the very icon
of human love in all her years
thesis and antithesis
bound together
inextricably by love

of fresh cut wildflowers that
turn a walk down a dirt road on a
humid afternoon into an april stroll
along the stone paved plaza of
the city of the gods
of a postcard in the mailbox with a
personal poem in which you
the lover
are a central character
about the gift that was selected
perfectly to suit the finest and
most private sensibilities of your heart
so pleasing that you could have
never selected it for yourself
that it had to be found by the most
sensitive amour under the most
objective and considerate conditions
within the most inspired
tenderness of imagination

it is about the love one knows
in the walled garden[4]

---

[4] *in that garden*
where the ancestors walk
and time
is a useless illusion
where peace or grief
as need be
sprouts and blossoms
and connects us with all things

                    where cynicism vanishes
and seclusion fosters love
without object
                    where there is no other
and resides a disincarnate
love for humanity animals birds plants
the sky god and earth
                    where scents and sounds blend with
                    memory and muse into
                    a sonatina of love

Bohpoli

who moved it? i shuddered

earth lay black
north wind tightened
its straightjacket grip
rattling cryptic limbs of oaks
quarter moon barely backlighting
sagging drapes of cloud

on my third trip for exercise
around midnight
stiff from reading rilke
to the cold steel barn
cold sleet hit my cheeks

as i walked the curving path
a hundred paces or so
through my chickasaw woods
squinting at flying ice
catching specks of light
i thought i felt a pebble
or an acorn hit the heel of my shoe
near a familiar
place on the trail

neck hairs bristled
the miniature metal folding chair
i had long ago painted white
suddenly appeared on the north
side of the path
its normal place was on the south

the chilling memory
of the missing child
a numb bell's toll
quickened my pace

i reasoned surely no one
would be out
on a night like this

---

*Bohpoli, or "the Thrower," is one of the Little People said to be responsible for all
the mysterious sounds heard in the woods. Bohpoli occasionally captures a child
and imparts secrets enabling that child to become alikchi, a doctor. Bohpoli also
assists in the gathering of forest herbs for the making of medicines.

Mobius Garden

my garden is
an exorbitant thing
luscious lavish passionate

wild unpredictable
chaotic like my youth
but fuller more resonant

tender top shoot
of a black-eyed pea vine
climbs the flaxen tassel
of a spent corn stalk
winding like a mobius strip
toward the top
heart-shaped embossed leaves
indigo green

yellow-copper purple
wine-red and green
in a striped pattern
almost shock the eye
as they appear on a corn leaf
two weeks after harvest

it is late summer
some things in my garden
are finished some still
fecund the grasses
weeds and wild vines
intermingled with
cultivated individuals
are mature also large
fat signature spiders
mount their webs
like lunar
landing modules

Vegetable River

i'm calling it the
        vegetable river since i'm planting
                curved lines tractor plow furrows
                        form the curves
                                ground so hard from drought
                                        it broke the heavy steel
                                        plow frame at a weld

                        but since plowing
                generous lugubrious rain squalls have
        penetrated the rigid earth and
softened it dramatically
        so that the seed
                now falls into cuddling humus

                        the vegetable river flows
                                around islands
                        in the narrow triangular plot
                perhaps a tenth part of an acre
        (big to work up by hand
but small by agrinomic measure)

    the tributary elliptical segments
        combine with the vegetable river
                to form the islands
                        tributaries of okra
                                flow into the mainstream
                of sweet corn beans and squash
        one island is mostly cowpeas
all islands have at least one giant sunflower
        two giant sunflower rows
                in the geographic center
                        form the mainland
                                at the extremity of the mainland

around which both forks flow
lies the delta
on the delta reside the melons
crimson sweet black diamond
and hale's best jumbos

the vegetable river moves slowly
like the nile
no rapids no falls
i am its floodplain
i am bottomland
i am fertile
i am rich

fire and wind

ripen the seed
aerate the soil
change the sea
to feather

soil to dust
mud and pulp to stone

seek and find
the turpentinous oils
and floral fibers
drafting the ash to smoke
returning them
to mix with *yakni*
and feed the seed

imagine themselves
in motion
like lightning
inside a river

dreaming their range
over hills
and peaks
with flesh
fleeing
flames
only
to return
and prosper
on the new grass

yakni = feminine
        life giving soul
        of the land

Fried Rabbit

The roadrunner reappeared
through broad jade leaves
hopping to a roosting perch on a cropped off
blackjack limb at eye level
15 feet behind my campfire

        wary bird
        this prairie recluse
        apparently relieved
        had been waiting to see
        what or whom
        I was going to eat

    no hunter no money
    living in a 1930's bus body
    on father *luak's* chickasaw land
    happy safe but hungry

    resiliently bright spring day[5]
    cleaning up the place
    sacred lamp lit

simmering skilleted rabbit with
fresh pulled carrots and beets
from poor carol's garden
fairylike birds dance
and sing their pleasure songs

---

[5] *if romance could be bought in packaged form*
what would the price tag be on an approaching storm
that mellows the sky over a rabbit feast
after a solitary day of work and peace

and what price the ticket on the show
starring scissortailed fly catchers
myself and an armadillo?
i'll pay i'll go

Digging Deeper

1. *The Secret Garden*

fooled the squash bugs
by setting young plants
in the center of piles
of old weathered cedar shingles
that i had dumped
one truckload at a time
around the perimeter of the woods
out of sight of the house
yet near enough to garner a hand
or bucketful for kindling
when the woodstove became
december's focus

the shingle pile had flattened
from firewood attrition and gravity
so only a few layers remained
no wild plants grew up through the shingles
although a couple of hours of sunshine
lit each pile each day
i called it the secret garden
because no one ever walks that way

ii. *The Change*

the middle vegetable garden
and the south garden (Vegetable River)
have provided entertainment and food

first the june-july drought
scorched and stunted growth
even with frequent watering
then came the late july
and august monsoons
with a 65–70/ 85–90 mix
almost every day

the plants invigorated
the bugs rebirthed
the grasses skyrocketed
from rock-hard drought
to rainforest jungle
i took a gas-powered weedeater
into the Vegetable River delta
yesterday whacked some high weeds
on the periphery of the melon patch
and uncovered two twenty-pound
crimson sweets in another corner
of the patch a crimson sweet was so ripe
that it had cracked itself open
sixty-five days after
sticking the seed in the ground

i was thrilled
after three years
of growing vines and stunted fruit
i had finally grown
big ripe melons

III. *August*

august gardening is by caesar
certainly august
the purple hulls the
yellow-shelled cowpeas
yellow and white okra blossoms
all wash out in the intensity
of <<green>> whelming <<green>>

even on a cool morning or evening
i come in from the search and harvest
having had not the slightest
perception of heat even with
sweat drenching my forehead
double-shirted long-sleeved
against the reborn mosquitoes
and realize only then
how hot my body is
the air is cool
what created the heat?

a perception narrows
that more than heat and humidity
are at play an intensity
a swollen vibration
more than the half-black over-ripe
jalapenos more than the
crisp prongs of okra pod
more than the nutty crunch
of raw cowpeas more than the
fruitful tangle of kentucky wonder and
morning glory smartweed vines
more than white glistening

corn smut blisters
more than the biggest brightest-marked
three-inch grasshoppers and cicadas
that you've ever seen
an intensity underlain in
a crush of   <<green>>   an interplay a
swollen vibration a
chlorophylandering that even
the dogs won't come near
no snakes no skinks no lizards
too strong for spiders

Before Dawn

there's a motion
outside
in the woods
the hills
it moves
like a fog
in the hollers

in the yip of yellow dogs

there's a motion
outside
in the trees
it's an acorn
cracking open ripe
the sound of the earth meeting sky

there's a motion
outside
it's a wiggle worm
in the soil
of the earth greeting sky

there's a motion
outside
it's unnameable
in the sound
between the earth
and the sky